The *SUPERPOWER* Field Guide

BEAVERS

BY **RACHEL POLIQUIN**

ILLUSTRATED BY
NICHOLAS JOHN FRITH

HOUGHTON MIFFLIN HARCOURT
Boston   New York

Dedicated to Humble Heroes everywhere.
You know who you are. —R.P.

To my family and friends, for believing in me and my
"paws of power." —N.J.F.

The author thanks the Canada Council for the Arts
for its generous support.

Text copyright © 2018 by Rachel Poliquin
Illustrations copyright © 2018 by Nicholas John Frith

hmhco.com

The illustrations in this book were produced using a mixture of black ink,
pencil, and wax crayon on paper, in a technique known as "preseparation."
For printing purposes here, the artwork was colored digitally.

The text type was set in Adobe Caslon Pro.
The display type was set in Sign Painter House Showcard.

Library of Congress Cataloging-in-Publication Data
Names: Poliquin, Rachel, 1975– author. | Frith, Nicholas John, illustrator.
Title: Beavers / by Rachel Poliquin ; illustrated by Nicholas John Frith.
Description: Boston : Houghton Mifflin Harcourt, [2018] | Series: The
superpower field guide | Audience: Age 7–10. | Audience: Grade 4 to 6.
Identifiers: LCCN 2017001211 | ISBN 9780544949874
Subjects: LCSH: Beavers—Juvenile literature.
Classification: LCC QL737.R632 P66 2018 | DDC 599.37—dc23
LC record available at https://lccn.loc.gov/2017001211

Manufactured in China
SCP 10 9 8 7 6 5 4 3 2 1
4500724379

THIS IS A BEAVER.

Just an ordinary beaver.

But even ordinary beavers are extraordinary. In fact, even ordinary beavers are superheroes.

Now, I can almost hear you saying, "But aren't beavers just lumpy rodents with buck teeth and funny flat tails?"

Yes, they are! And believe it or not, those buck teeth and funny flat tails are just a few of the things that make beavers extraordinary.

"Impossible!" you say.

I say, "You don't know beavers."

But you will.

MEET ELMER

MEET ELMER, AN ORDINARY BEAVER. He may not be as majestic as a lion or as ferocious as a shark. He may be lumpy, squat, and brown. But never underestimate a humble hero like Elmer. His beaver superpowers include:

CHAINSAW TEETH

UNSTOPPABLE FUR

EVER-TOILING TAIL

THE INCREDIBLE SCUBA HEAD

HYDROPOWERED BUILDING BRILLIANCE

PAWS OF POWER

SUBAQUATIC WINTER SIEGE SURVIVAL SKILLS

TURBOCHARGED SUPERSTINK

INDUBITABLE DELUGE DOMINATION
(That means Elmer is King of the Floods!)

UNBEATABLE BOGMAKER

And that's not all—what an ordinary beaver can do with his superpowered parts put together is Unthinkable! Unstoppable! Utterly Gobsmackable!

So sit back, relax, and allow me to explain the amazing powers of **ELMER, WETLAND WARRIOR!**

KNOW YOUR RODENTS

FIRST LET'S MEET ELMER'S FAMILY: *rodents!*

BEAVERS are rodents.

so are **PORCUPINES** . . .

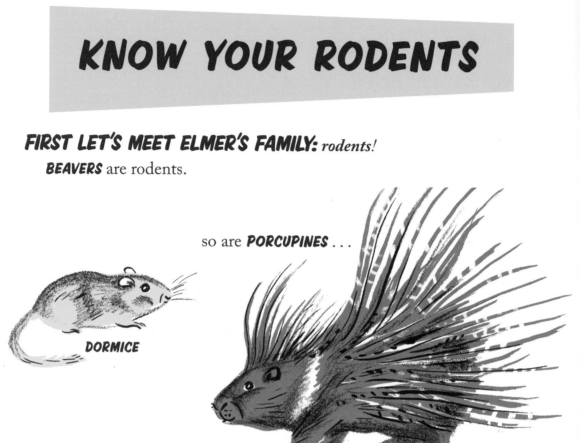

DORMICE

RATS

HAMSTERS

MICE

CHINCHILLAS

NOTE: Rodents not drawn to scale.

The word *rodent* means **"THE BEAST THAT GNAWS."** And it is true. All rodents (except one) chew furiously at anything they can find. Beavers gnaw down trees. Squirrels break open nuts, and porcupines chew right through metal park signs that say "Don't Feed the Porcupines."

Why do rodents chew so much? Good question. They don't have a choice. They have to keep chewing . . . **OR THEY'LL DIE.**

You see, all rodents (except one) have two upper front teeth and two lower front teeth called *incisors* that continue to grow throughout the animal's life. Imagine that: **EVER-GROWING TEETH.** And all rodents (except one) keep those teeth short and sharp by chewing. When rodents gnaw, their upper and lower incisors slice and grind against each other like a pair of scissors. The more a rodent chews, the more its teeth slice and grind, and the sharper they become.

But ever-growing teeth can become a horrible problem. If Elmer were to lose an upper incisor, his lower tooth could continue to grow in an upward curve until it pierced his skull. Poor Elmer—let's hope he doesn't chip a tooth!

All rodents (except one) also have grinding molars at the back. The exception? *Paucidentomys vermidax*, or "few-toothed worm-eating mouse," has two upper teeth and two lower teeth, but they aren't ever-growing, so this mouse can't gnaw. It lives in Indonesia on a strict diet of earthworms.

3 INCHES (7.5 CM)

Beaver incisors are three inches (7.6 centimeters) long and bright orange.

Now, I know bright orange teeth don't sound as impressive as x-ray vision or freezing breath, but never underestimate a beaver's bite. Those big orange teeth are **ELMER'S FIRST SUPERPOWER.**

SUPERPOWER #1
CHAINSAW TEETH

BEAVERS CAN SNAP A TREE as thick as your arm in two or three bites. They can chew through a tree trunk as thick as your body in less than an hour. And in a week or so, even an ordinary beaver like Elmer can take down a tree as wide as your leg is long.

How do beavers chew so much, so quickly? Another good question. Let's explore the **MECHANICS OF SUPERPOWERED MUNCHING**.

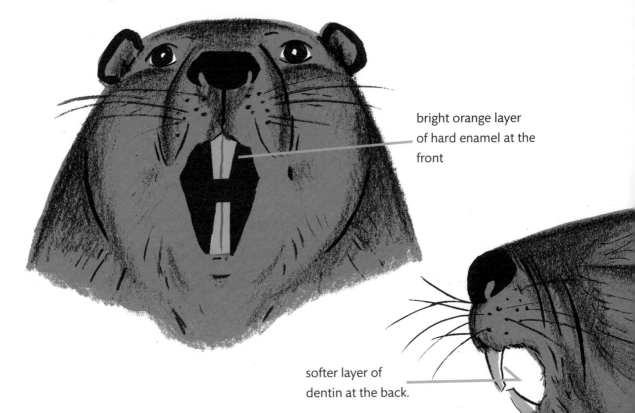

bright orange layer of hard enamel at the front

softer layer of dentin at the back.

The *dentin* layer wears away faster than the *enamel* one to create a razor-sharp edge on Elmer's teeth. Elmer also has a massive head and powerful jaw muscles to give his bite chainsaw power.

An ancient Roman named Pliny the Elder wrote that if beavers get ahold of a man's body, "they will never let go until his bones are broken and crackle under their teeth." Not true. But beavers do have a fierce bite. How could they not, with such big teeth? So don't poke the beaver.

Let's watch as Elmer approaches an aspen tree, one of his favorites.

STEP 1: First Elmer bites
out a chunk of bark.

STEP 3: Elmer continues in
circles, going around and
around the tree, gnawing a
deeper and deeper ring . . .

STEP 2: Then he turns his head sideways, bites into the cut, and twists his head straight.

That twisting motion creates enough force to tear out a large strip of wood.

STEP 4: until the tree topples over.

KNOW YOUR BEAVERS

ELMER LIVES WITH HIS LIFELONG PARTNER—let's call her Irma—in a pond they built together in the northern wilderness of British Columbia. (That's in Canada.) Elmer and Irma have been together for six years already. Beavers are very faithful partners.

Elmer and Irma live with their four baby beavers, called *kits*, and three yearlings that were born last year. Next spring, the yearlings will leave home to start their own families. The kits will grow into yearlings, and Irma will have another litter of baby beavers. And so life will continue pleasantly for years—beavers can live to be twenty-four years old.

Okay, here's a question: If you look very closely at Elmer and Irma, can you tell which is Elmer and which is Irma? No? Don't worry. Neither can I.

Male and female beavers look exactly the same, from the outside. And beavers get even more confusing.

If you were to dig a hole at the bottom of Elmer's pond and continue digging and digging through the earth, you would probably melt when you got to the center. But if you didn't melt, and if you kept on digging and digging and digging, you might pop out somewhere in Russia. And if you did, you might meet another beaver family on the other side of the world.

You see, there are, in fact, two beaver species. One lives in North America. It's called the **NORTH AMERICAN BEAVER.** The other lives in Europe and Asia. Guess what it's called? **THE EURASIAN BEAVER.** Not very imaginative names, but at least they're easy to remember.

> Scientists call North American beavers *Castor canadensis. Castor* is Greek for "beaver" and *canadensis* is just a fancy way of saying "from Canada." Eurasian beavers are called *Castor fiber.* Now, since *fiber* is the Latin word for beaver and *castor* is Greek for beaver, *Castor fiber* means "beaver beaver," which is ridiculous but *really* easy to remember.

So if we put all four beavers together—Elmer and Irma and Boris and Tatyana (those are the Russian beavers)—can you tell who is who this time?

Still no?

Nobody can. Nobody even knew for sure that Eurasian and North American beavers were different species until scientists tested beaver DNA in the 1970s. Scientists think the two beaver species were separated seven million years ago, which is a very long time.

North American beavers live throughout Canada and the United States from the Pacific Ocean to the Atlantic Ocean. But you won't find any beavers in the Arctic (no trees), the deserts of the United States (no trees or water), or Florida (alligator-infested waters!). They live in a few other places too, but I'll explain that in a bit.

The Eurasian beaver used to live throughout Eurasia from England to Mongolia and from the northern tip of Norway all the way south into Turkey. But that was a very long time ago. For a while, it was nearly impossible to find a Eurasian beaver anywhere in Eurasia. They almost went extinct. North American beavers almost went extinct as well. And it was because beaver fur is superpowered!

SUPERPOWER #2

UNSTOPPABLE FUR

MOST ANIMALS THAT LIVE in northern parts of the world have thick fur to keep them warm in the winter, and beavers are no exception. Beaver fur has up to 100,000 hairs per square inch (20,000 hairs per square centimeter). Your head has about 1,000 hairs per square inch (20 hairs per square centimeter). So if you grew a beaver on your head, each of your hairs would sprout into 100 hairs. Talk about having a hot head!

Like most hairy animals, beavers have two kinds of fur. Their **guard hairs** are chestnut brown, long, and silky, and their underfur is short, thick, gray, and fuzzy.

And that is precisely why beavers almost went extinct—everyone wanted to wear a beaver on their head. I know that sounds crazy, but it's true. Well, not living beavers. Beaver hats. Or to be perfectly precise, beaver-felt hats. And *felt* is the all-important word.

You can make felt from any kind of fur or wool. Just boil it until the hairs mat together to form a dense fabric. Sheep felt is probably the most common. Goat hair makes a good felt hat. Camel felt makes a sturdy desert tent. But beaver felt . . . you know what I'm going to say, right? Beaver felt is the toughest, strongest, best-est felt ever!

COMMON

GOOD

STURDY

BEST-EST EVER

It might not stop a speeding bullet, but a hat made from **UNSTOPPABLE FUR** is strong enough to survive lashing rain, blowing snow, and a hard day's gallop.

You see, each hair of beaver *underfur* is covered with dozens of tiny barbs like fishhooks. When millions of beaver hairs mat together, millions and millions of tiny fishhooks hook together to make beaver felt superpowered.

Wool bonnets sag in the rain. Goat-felt caps flop. Even leather hats slump. But the brims of beaver hats never droop! Beaver crowns never sag! Beaver hats stand tall and proud!

Think of all the famous hats in history.

Napoleon's bicorn hat?
BEAVER!

A pilgrim's cockle hat?
BEAVER!

A gentleman's top hat?
BEAVER!

The Three Musketeers' plumed chapeaux?
BEAVER! BEAVER! BEAVER!

Gosh . . . I got excited about beaver hats, didn't I? Sorry. I won't let it happen again. But beaver hats are amazing. In fact, they were the main reason Europeans came to North America in the early seventeenth century.

You see, Eurasian beavers were almost extinct throughout Europe and Asia, and beaver fur was in short supply. But Canada was teeming with beavers. The United States was thick with beavers. Even northern parts of Mexico were overrun with beavers. There were so many beavers, you couldn't throw a beaver without hitting a beaver, if you'll pardon the expression. No one knows how many beavers once lived in North America. Some say 50 million. Some say 200 million.

But by the early nineteenth century, so many beavers had been killed in North America to make hats that beavers were harder to find than a mole in the ocean, and believe me, that's hard to find. And it was all because of their **UNSTOPPABLE FUR.**

And did you know beaver felt was the reason the Mad Hatter was so dotty in the head? You see, beaver felt was made by a process called *carroting*. Carroting meant soaking beaver furs in mercury. The mercury opened up the fur's barbs and made the felt extra strong. But the process wasn't perfect. It tinted the felt orange, like a carrot. Worse, mercury gives off toxic fumes. Spending all day breathing mercury fumes will bake your brains and addle your noodle. And that's why we say someone is "mad as a hatter"!

But I won't ramble on about hats. I'll just finish by saying beavers are doing just fine now. I mean, have you seen anyone wearing a top hat lately?

By 1900, only 1,200 Eurasian beavers and 100,000 North American beavers were left alive. But with a little help from scientists and some serious superbeaver grit, beavers are back! There are now more than one million Eurasian beavers and more than 15 million North American beavers.

WORLD BEAVER MAP

IF YOU SEE A BEAVER IN CALIFORNIA or Quebec, you know it's a North American beaver. And if you see a beaver in Russia or France, you know it's a Eurasian beaver. Right?

Wrong. North American beavers are globetrotters!

You see, before scientists knew there were two beaver species, they captured some North American beavers and let them loose in beaver-barren rivers in Europe, Scandinavia, and Russia. The beavers loved their new homes! But once scientists discovered the new beavers were a different species, they weren't so happy about all those North American beavers chewing and chomping their way through Eurasian forests. If the invading beavers took the best rivers and chewed the best trees, they might spread until there was no room for their Eurasian cousins. But invading beavers are casuing even more trouble at the bottom of the world.

In 1946, someone had the not-so-great idea of starting a beaver fur trade on the islands at the southern tip of South America. Twenty North American beavers were let loose. But the fur trade flopped, and the beavers were forgotten.

But beavers are survivors. If you give them enough wood and water, they can do almost anything. By 2008, those twenty beavers had turned into an ever-growing horde of 200,000 chomping beavers!

And here's the problem: the southern beech trees have never been chewed by beavers before, and they don't like it. And they don't like wet roots, either. But the beavers keep swimming from island to island, chomping and flooding, and the trees aren't growing back. The beavers are causing so much damage that scientists are planning ways to remove them to save the *ecology* of the islands.

BEAVER MAP FACTS AND LOCATIONS

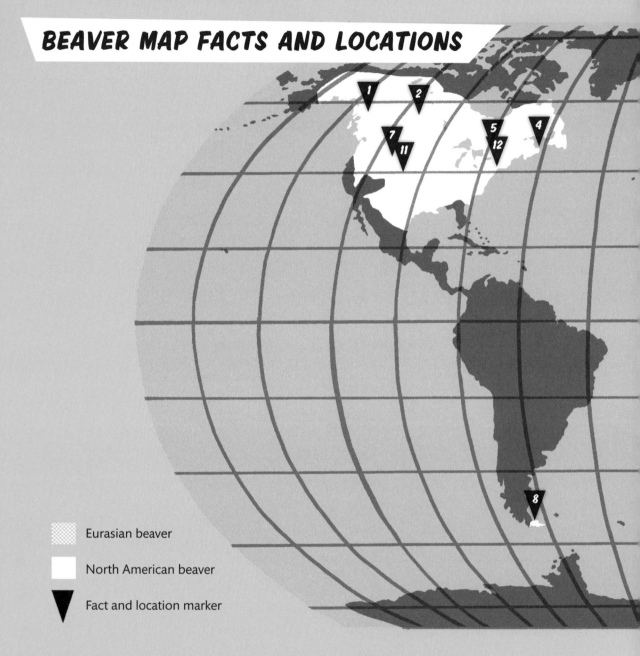

Eurasian beaver

North American beaver

Fact and location marker

1. Elmer and Irma's home.

2. The world's largest beaver dam.

3. Ancient doctors claimed that beaver stink from Turkish beavers made the best medicines.

4. North America's first fur-trading post established at Sable Island in 1598. This was a bad day for North American beavers.

5. The first beaver sanctuary was established in

1836 on Carleton Island by the Hudson's Bay Company, the largest fur-trading company ever.

6. Thirty beavers living in France were one of eight lonely beaver populations that were used to reintroduce beavers into Eurasian rivers.

7. In 1948, the Idaho Fish and Game Commission airdropped seventy-six beavers in crates with parachutes to repopulate the forest with beavers. The crazy plan worked!

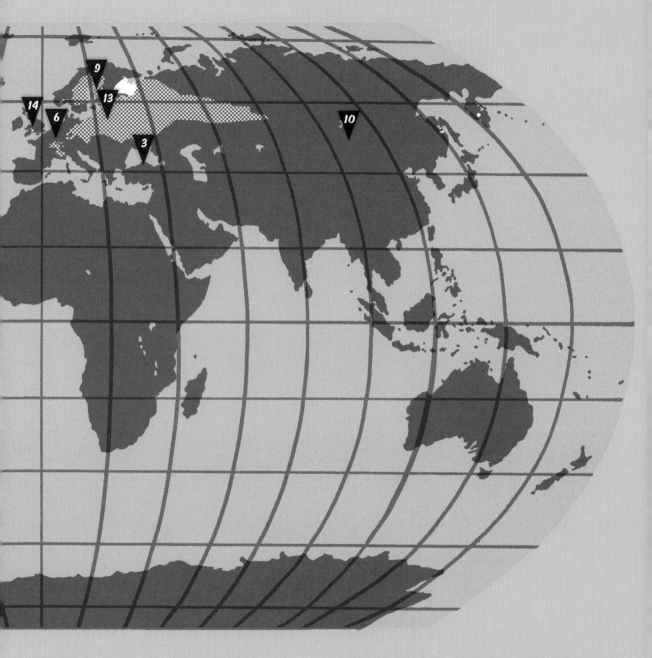

8. In 1946, twenty North American beavers were set free on Isla Grande in Tierra del Fuego on the southern tip of South America. This was a very, very bad idea.

9. Ninety percent of Finland's 12,000 beavers are descended from seven North American beavers released in 1937.

10. In 2012, forty-four beavers from Germany and Russia were sent to Mongolia to restore their rivers and wetlands.

11. The Grand Canyon Trust has reintroduced beavers into eighty beaver-barren rivers on the Colorado Plateau in southern Utah.

12. Home of José and Justin Beaver.

13. In 2013, a man in Belarus died after being bitten in the leg by a beaver.

14. In 2014, a family of beavers was spotted on the River Otter in Devon County—the first wild beavers seen in England in more than five hundred years!

HOW'D ELMER GET SO BIG?

SO FAR YOU KNOW ELMER is a *Castor canadensis* with **CHAINSAW TEETH** and **UNSTOPPABLE FUR**. The next thing you need to know about Elmer is that he is big. Maybe not as big as Superman, but he's bigger than you might think.

From the tip of his nose to the end of his tail, Elmer is 52 inches (132 centimeters) long and weighs just a little over 48 pounds (22 kilograms). Are you bigger than a beaver? But beavers can get much bigger. The biggest beaver on record weighed more than 110 pounds (50 kilograms). He lived in the Iron River in Wisconsin.

Beavers are big, but they aren't the biggest rodents. The capybara is even bigger. It can weigh up to 200 pounds (90 kilograms).

BROWN BEAR

BUFFALO

HUMPBACK WHALE

So what does Elmer eat to get so big? Brown bears? Buffalo? Humpback whales? Of course not! Elmer is a vegetarian. His favorite meal is the *underbark* of trees—that's the green layer between the tree and its outer woody bark. Elmer likes aspen, birch, maple, and cherry.

ASPEN

BIRCH

MAPLE

CHERRY

ORDER HERE!

He also eats water lilies, pondweeds, and maybe an apple or two, but the soft underbark of trees is really the best.

After Elmer chews down a tree, he strips off all the bark and eats the tender bits. If the branch is small, he'll hold it in his front paws and nibble around and around like you might eat an ear of corn, only at turbo speed and with much less butter.

After his meal, maybe Elmer rests a little. Who knows? It doesn't matter. What matters is what Elmer does next with that branch . . .

He builds himself a home.

Did you hear what I just said? Elmer builds a home with his leftovers! That's like a seagull who gobbles up a hundred clams and then makes herself a cottage with their shells. Or imagine your dad buys a window to replace the broken one in the kitchen. The new window arrives in a cardboard box. If you were a family of beavers, you'd eat that box.

Crazy! But also super-amazingly sensible, when you think about it. Elmer spends hours chewing down trees. Gnawing is hard work, and Elmer probably gets tired and hungry. If Elmer ate huckleberries or skunks, he would have to hunt down huckleberries or skunks after a day of hard chewing, and that would be double the work. Instead Elmer can nibble while he gnaws.

While on the subject of food, I should mention something else that beavers eat. But I won't make you guess, because you'll never guess. Are you ready?

Beavers eat their own **_droppings_**, and droppings, as you might know, is a polite word for animal poop.

I know what you're thinking . . . _Why on earth would Elmer do such a thing?_

It is a very good question. Perhaps your best question yet.

Let me quickly say that it is not quite as gross as it sounds. Because beavers eat so much bark, beaver droppings are really just balls of wood chips and sawdust. But I will admit that poop eating is definitely too gross to be a superpower.

PICK UP YOUR LITTER

NOT A SUPERPOWER: POOP EATING

THE REASON ELMER EATS HIS DROPPINGS is that wood and bark need several passes through his digestive system before they break down. When I say "break down," I don't mean like that time your uncle's car caught fire. Your digestive system breaks down food so that your body can absorb and use the nutrients. Some foods are harder to break down than others are. And wood, as you can imagine, is particularly hard to digest.

Most animals that eat *roughage* (which means super-high-fiber food like wood, grass, and hay) have special digestive systems. Cows have four stomachs to help break down all the grass they eat. Horses have enormously long guts that can stretch to more than 100 feet long (31 meters). That's the length of three school buses!

And beavers eat their droppings. And it is all because cows, horses, and beavers eat so much roughage.

But enough about guts and roughage and poop eating. Let's change the subject. Besides, it's time for your **FIRST QUIZ.** I bet you didn't see that coming, did you?

QUIZ #1

PLEASE ANSWER TRUE OR FALSE.

1. A capybara has a North American beaver for a father and a Eurasian beaver for a mother.

2. Scientists call beavers that live in Utah *Castor utahensis* and beavers that live in Mexico *Castor mexicanus.* Beavers that live in New York City are called José and Justin Beaver.

3. Men who wear beaver top hats are taller than men without hats.

4. Beaver teeth are sharp enough to cut an alligator in half.

5. Beavers are such excellent diggers, Russian prisoners train beavers to dig escape tunnels out of jail.

1. **FALSE.** North American beavers and Eurasian beavers don't just live on different continents. They are completely different species, which means they are not able to mate. And even if they could, they certainly wouldn't raise baby capybaras. That's just silly.

2. **FALSE.** All North American beavers, whether they live in Utah, Mexico, Alaska, or Canada, are the same species. They are all *Castor canadensis*. **BUT IT IS TRUE** that two beavers living in the Bronx River in New York City are named José and Justin Beaver. No beavers had been seen in the Bronx River for more than two hundred years. But then, in 2007, a lone beaver appeared. No one knows where he came from. Nobody even knows whether he is a "he" (as I said, all beavers look exactly alike). The beaver got the nickname José after the politician José E. Serrano, who raised money to clean up the river. In 2008, a second beaver arrived and was nicknamed Justin Beaver after the singer Justin Bieber.

3. **TRUE.** Of course it's true. If you had a pineapple on your head, you would be taller than if you didn't. Same goes for a beaver top hat, which, for the record, is about as tall as a pineapple.

4. **TRUE.** I doubt anyone has tried to cut an alligator in half with a beaver tooth, but I guess it would be possible . . . as long as the alligator didn't cut you in half first! Indigenous peoples of North America used beaver incisors as knives and picks. They tied the tooth to a bone or wood handle and used it to cut anything that needed cutting.

5. **FALSE.** I didn't say beavers dug that tunnel through the earth! It was a *hypothetical* tunnel I was using to make a point. No Russians have ever trained beavers to dig escape tunnels. At least no Russians I know. But beavers are very good at digging. With long, sharp claws on their front paws, beavers can dig tunnels as fast as a small man with a large shovel. You'll see.

IT'S A GOOSE!
IT'S A FISH!
IT'S ELMER!

Lots of superheroes have double identities. Take Clark Kent . . . He has a stoop; he's thin; he even mumbles a bit. Yet hidden within mumbly Clark Kent is Superman!

The same is true with beavers. On land, Elmer is pudgy and podgy and waddles like a big fat goose. But put Elmer into water and he's as graceful as a dolphin. He's smoother than a minnow. He dives through the water with the greatest of ease. Elmer comes alive in water, and from the tip of his nose to the end of his tail, Elmer's most amazing features are made for his watery life.

Let's start with Elmer's hard-working tail.

SUPERPOWER #3

EVER-TOILING TAIL

NO ANIMAL HAS ANYTHING like a beaver's tail.
Beaver tails are . . .

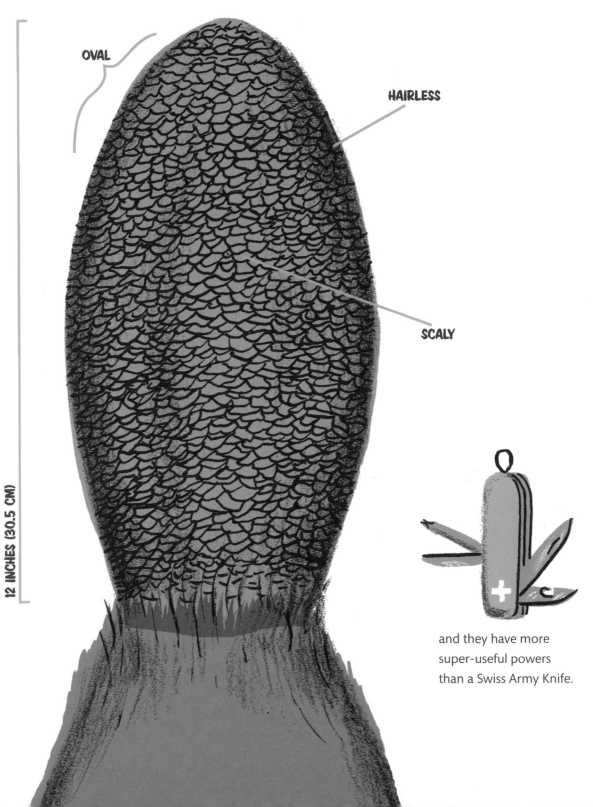

OVAL

HAIRLESS

SCALY

12 INCHES (30.5 CM)

and they have more super-useful powers than a Swiss Army Knife.

FIRST: It is an enormous flipper that helps Elmer swim and dive like a fish.

SECOND: It is a kickstand that helps Elmer balance while he chews down trees. It also helps him waddle along on his hind feet. That's right . . . Elmer can walk upright on two legs! But more on that later.

THIRD: It is a danger whistle. At the first whiff of trouble, Elmer slaps his tail on water—*wafffftttttt!*—to warn his family.

FOURTH: It is a fat reserve, which means Elmer stores up fat in his tail during the summer and burns the fat in the winter to keep himself warm. Elmer's tail will be half the size by the end of winter as it was at the beginning.

FIFTH: It's also a thermoregulator, which means it helps beavers control their body temperature. Let me explain. Elmer's thick fur keeps him warm in icy-winter waters. But Elmer can't take off his fur coat in summer. Instead he takes long, cool swims in his pond, and his hairless tail really helps get rid of extra heat.

That's five amazing things Elmer's tail can do! I mean, what has your dog's tail done lately? Wag? Pfft.

Next up, **BEAVER SCUBA GEAR!**

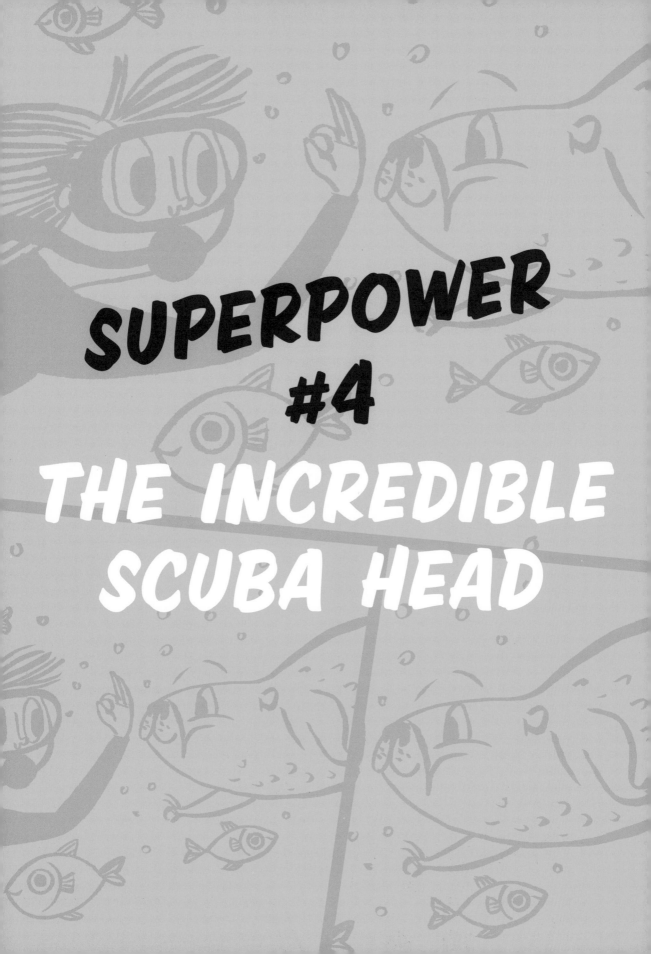

SUPERPOWER
#4

THE INCREDIBLE
SCUBA HEAD

FIRST OFF, ELMER CAN HOLD his breath underwater for fifteen minutes.

What? You don't think that's impressive?

Okay. Did you know Elmer was born with swimming goggles? That's right. Elmer has transparent eyelids that cover his eyeballs when he is underwater. They don't close up and down, like your eyelids, but sideways across his eyeballs. (Elmer still has eyelids like yours that close when he sleeps.) Scientists call them *nictitating membranes,* but I call them **UNDERWATER GOGGLE GREATNESS!** Nictitating membranes help Elmer see perfectly underwater and protect his eyes from mud and grit in the water.

NICTITATING MEMBRANES

And then there's Elmer's **BEAVER STEALTH-SWIMMING TECHNIQUE.** Elmer's eyes, ears, and nose are high on his head, so he can swim with just the tippy-top of his head out of the water. That means he can hear, smell, and see you, but you'll probably miss him as he glides silently by.

And what about the watertight valves in his nose and ears?
Elmer's got those, too. They seal shut when he dives underwater.

Elmer also has fur-lined lips, which close behind his incisors so that
he can swim with branches in his teeth or chew wood underwater.

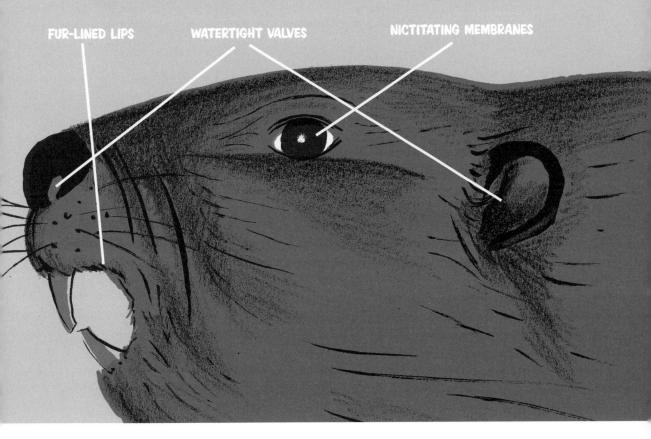

FUR-LINED LIPS   **WATERTIGHT VALVES**   **NICTITATING MEMBRANES**

And then there are Elmer's webbed hind feet. After all, what good is a scuba head without a pair of flippers?

With each flippered kick, Elmer shoots through the water faster than an Olympic swimmer—about 5 miles (8 kilometers) an hour.

But what's even more impressive than his **EVER-TOILING TAIL** and his **INCREDIBLE SCUBA HEAD** is how Elmer puts all his superpowers together to build himself a home.

CAPTAIN COLIN COMICS

3

1

2

SUPERPOWER
#5

HYDROPOWERED
BUILDING
BRILLIANCE

LET'S IMAGINE THE BEAUTIFUL summer day when Elmer and Irma first arrived in their forest. It is a lovely forest with a stream running through it—a very pleasant spot indeed. But if Elmer and Irma are going to make this forest their home, they need to turn that trickling stream into a wide and roomy pond to keep their family safe.

You see, lots of animals like bears, wolves, and cougars think Elmer looks terrifically plump and tasty. True, Elmer has a fierce bite, but he is slow and lumbering on land. He's a lover, not a fighter. He would much rather slip into his pond as quickly as possible and thumb his nose at that bear. But if the pond is shallow, that bear could wade in after Elmer and gobble him up. That means Elmer needs lots of water, and quick!

Elmer doesn't just hope for rain. And he doesn't use a garden hose to fill up his pond. Real heroes don't wait for things to happen. Real heroes get busy and *make* things happen. And Elmer can make water happen! Lots and lots of water. As much water as his family could ever want! And here's how he does it:

STEP 1: CHEW

First Elmer needs to build a dam across the stream. And to build a dam, he needs logs. And to get logs, he needs to start chewing. Elmer and Irma begin gnawing, Elmer working on his tree and Irma chewing on hers. Beavers don't usually gnaw the same tree at the same time, but they do enjoy working side by side. If they weren't so busy gnawing, I bet Elmer and Irma would whistle a jolly tune. But it is hard to whistle with wood chips in your teeth.

STEP 2: DRAG

Once the trees are down, Elmer and Irma break off the branches (to make the log easier to move) and eat the underbark (yum!). If the log is too big, they chew it into handy-size sections. Then they drag the logs into the water with their teeth and swim to just the right spot for a dam.

Remember those fur-lined lips? They let Irma swim with a tree in her mouth without choking on great gobs of water. And those enormous webbed feet and big flipper tail? They give Elmer the superpower to kick while dragging heavy logs through the water. And remember how beavers' ears, eyes, and noses are high up on their heads? They let Elmer and Irma swim along almost invisibly while branches seem to move themselves through the water.

STEP 3: ARRANGE

Irma and Elmer drag logs to just the right part of the river and start building. Sometimes Irma sticks one end of a branch into the bottom of the stream. Sometimes Elmer just lays the branch sideways at the bottom—it depends on how deep the water is and how fast the stream is flowing. Then back to chewing another tree, and another, and another. Elmer and Irma build the dam higher and higher, weaving logs and branches together to make a large and solid structure.

STEP 4: PAT

A big pile of logs won't stop water from flowing through all the cracks. The next step is mud. Elmer dives down to the bottom of the river and scoops up a big armload of mud. Elmer's swimming goggles are especially helpful for this job. It's murky down there. Elmer wouldn't want to scoop up a trout by mistake.

Then, with his armload of mud, Elmer swims to the dam and waddles up the side on his hind legs, carrying the mud in his arms. He plops the mud down and pats it down into all the cracks and gaps with his front paws. When the mud hardens, the dam will be watertight.

A family of beavers can make a small dam overnight. But if you give beavers time, they can make a dam that's visible from space! It's true—the biggest beaver dam on record is 2,800 feet (850 meters) long. It's in Wood Buffalo National Park in northern Alberta, Canada. If you flipped that dam upright, it would stand as tall as the Great Pyramid of Giza stacked on top of the Eiffel Tower stacked on top of the Empire State Building!

2,800 FEET (850 METERS)

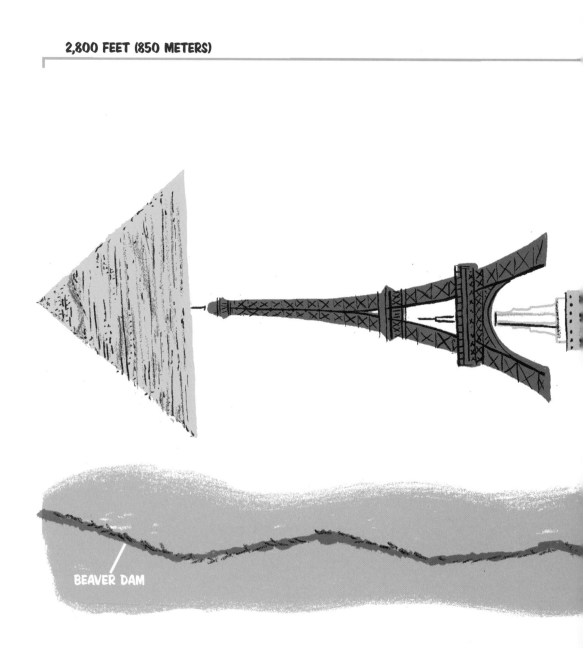

BEAVER DAM

As I said, never underestimate a beaver—and I'm not finished yet.

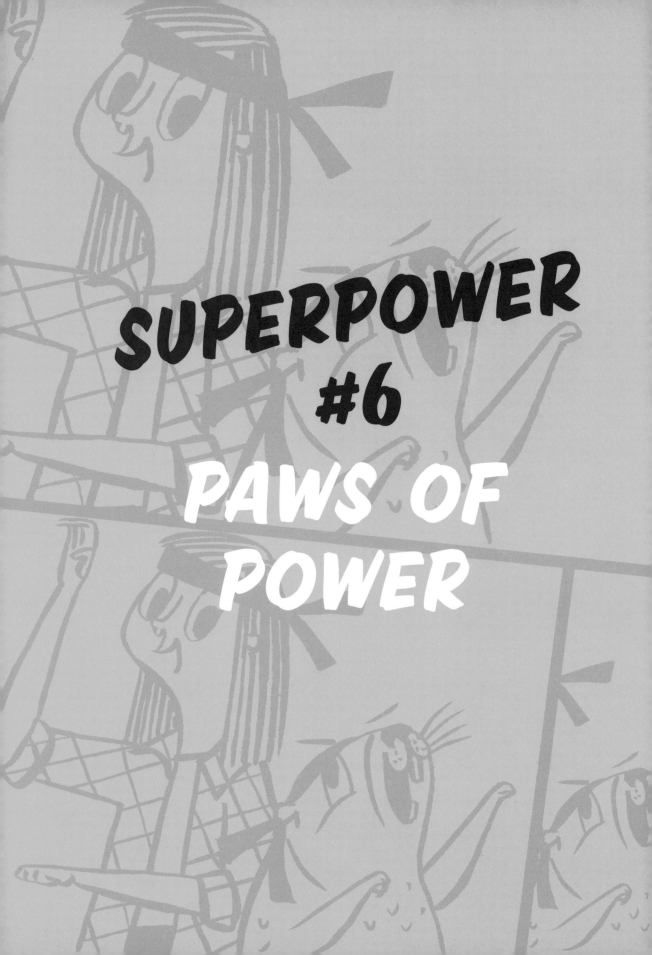

SUPERPOWER #6

PAWS OF POWER

WHAT'S THE BIGGEST CLUE there's a beaver about?

Stumps!

If you see a lake filled with stumps, you know a family of beavers has been busy. And the busier the beavers, the more trees they chew. Which means soon Elmer and Irma will have munched down all the trees around their pond.

Elmer can see a tasty clump of trees about a quarter mile away. He sniffs the air; is that the smell of bear? Maybe there is a cougar about.

Even if Elmer is brave enough to leave the safety of his pond and waddle overland to the trees, and even if no bears hear him chewing, and even if he does chew down the tree, how does he get it back to the dam?

Elmer is strong and sturdy, but dragging a log through the forest is hard work. What if he had to pull it uphill? What if the log got stuck on another tree? What if a bear heard the racket and came to see who was causing all the fuss? Elmer needs a better way to get those trees to his pond than the **DANGEROUS OVERLAND WADDLE.**

Remember Elmer's little front paws? They spring into superhero action. Those paws may be little, but they're **PAWS OF POWER!**

Elmer and Irma begin digging a trench from their pond. They dig and dig, pile the mud alongside the trench, then dig and dig some more. They'll dig until they have a canal all the way to that clump of tasty trees. And when they've chewed down those trees, Elmer and Irma will dig more canals to more clumps of trees.

Beavers build water highways through the forest so they can swim to any tree they want. That means Elmer can slip into the water if he hears a bear sniffing about, no matter how far he is from his pond. And canals make moving logs easy. You know how everything is lighter in water? Why struggle and grunt uphill with a heavy log when you can paddle pleasantly using the *BEAVER STEALTH-SWIMMING TECHNIQUE?*

RIVER SOURCE

CANAL

CANAL

CANAL

BEAVER POND

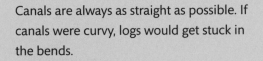
Canals are always as straight as possible. If canals were curvy, logs would get stuck in the bends.

LODGE

CANAL

CANAL

DAM

DIRECTION OF RIVER FLOW

JUST A QUICK NOTE

ELMER IS THE HERO of this book, but I want to make something very clear. Every time I say that Elmer chews a tree, or Elmer builds a dam, or Elmer digs up mud, I could just as well say Irma chews, Irma builds, Irma digs.

Not only do Elmer and Irma look exactly alike, they do everything together. If you visited their pond and saw one beaver digging a canal and another patting mud, you would have absolutely no idea which beaver was Irma and which was Elmer.

HOME IS WHERE I WANT TO BE

ONCE THE STREAM IS DAMMED and the pond begins to grow, Elmer and Irma start building their home. A beaver's home is called a *lodge.* Don't ask me why. It looks more like a cabin to me.

Building a lodge is much the same as building a dam. It goes something like this: chew, gnaw, chew, gnaw, drag, swim, drag, arrange, scoop, pat, scoop, pat.

Repeat.

Repeat.

Repeat.

It might take Elmer and Irma three weeks to build their lodge. That's a lot of gnawing! Good thing beavers have **CHAINSAW TEETH**.

STEP 1: They begin by stacking logs and branches in the middle of the pond.

STEP 3: A beaver's lodge can be 40 feet across, 10 feet high (12 meters x 3 meters), and it can have more than three tons of logs and mud! It's so strong, even a bear couldn't break in!

STEP 2: The mound grows up from the bottom, sort of like a big wooden triangle with more and more branches and more and more mud to make the walls solid.

STEP 4: So here is a question. If a big bear can't break in, how do Elmer and Irma get inside?

Can you guess?

Elmer and Irma chew their way into their home!

Once the lodge is finished, Elmer and Irma begin chewing an opening underwater. They keep chewing upward until they are above the water level. Then they chew out one or two large rooms inside the lodge. One to sleep in and one for birthday parties and other special events. (That's not true, but I like the idea of beavers wearing party hats.)

They cover the floor with reeds and grasses to make nice soft beds. And then do you know what Elmer and Irma are going to do?

Sleep.

Elmer and Irma will probably sleep the entire day away. But then, they usually sleep their days away. Beavers are mostly *nocturnal*, which means they mostly work at night. But enough talking. Let's let Elmer and Irma sleep. They deserve it.

TIME FOR YOUR SECOND QUIZ.

QUIZ #2

PLEASE ANSWER TRUE OR FALSE.

1. Elmer will die if his tail dries out because his tail is actually a trout.

2. Elmer is better at the doggy paddle, but Irma is the queen of the backstroke.

3. Elmer and Irma sometimes rent out rooms in their lodge to muskrats, visiting voles, and other such folk.

4. Giant prehistoric beavers built the Egyptian pyramids.

5. Beavers love the sound of running water. Elmer even whittled himself a banjo so he could strum as the water trickles through his dam.

ANSWERS:

1. **FALSE.** That's silly. Who thinks of such things? A beaver is 100 percent beaver.

2. **FALSE.** Beavers don't use their front paws while swimming. They let them dangle by their sides while their tail and webbed hind feet do all the hard work.

3. **TRUE.** Can you believe it? If there is room available, beavers don't mind sharing their homes with a muskrat or two. They even charge rent, of sorts. I once saw a muskrat take out the dirty bedding and replace it with clean reeds.

4. **FALSE.** But giant prehistoric beavers did exist! The beavers were as big as black bears, weighed more than 200 pounds (90 kilograms), and had teeth that were more than six inches (15 centimeters) long. They died out 10,000 years ago at the end of the last ice age, along with other such enormous, hairy, big-toothed creatures as mammoths and saber-toothed tigers.

5. **FALSE.** The sound of running water drives beavers crazy! If Elmer hears running water, it means there is a leak in the dam. The whole family springs into action to fix the leak.

WHERE'S ELMER?

YOU KNOW A LOT about beavers now. You know Elmer uses his **CHAINSAW TEETH** and **HYDROPOWERED BUILDING BRILLIANCE** to build his family a watery home. You know that Elmer digs canals with his **PAWS OF POWER** so that he can swim to the tastiest trees without worrying about beaver-eating bears. And you know that Elmer sleeps most days and works most nights to keep his dam and lodge in tiptop shape. In other words, you know Elmer and his family have worked hard all summer!

But their work isn't done yet. The leaves are turning red and orange, and the nights are getting chilly. Winter is coming, and winter in northern Canada is particularly fierce and cold.

Most northern animals have some sort of winter ritual. Geese and ducks fly south to warmer lands. Bears gorge on blueberries until they're fat enough to sleep through winter. Squirrels hide peanuts in your flower garden. But not beavers. Beavers don't fly south. They don't hibernate. And they certainly don't like peanuts. Instead beavers do something especially clever.

Now, to understand what's so clever, let me paint you a picture of your visit . . . yes, that's right—*your* visit to Elmer's pond. Let's say it's February 17, one of the coldest days of the year. It is −30°F. You're going to need some supplies.

If you don't already have one, borrow a **PARKA WITH A HOOD.**

Then tie a **SCARF** around your face—it will keep your nostrils from freezing together.

You'll need **FLEECE-LINED GLOVES,**

SNOWSHOES,

SNOW BOOTS, that lace up to your knees,

and the warmest **THERMAL UNDERWEAR** money can buy.

Elmer's pond isn't anywhere near a road, but you can catch a ride with my friend and his dogsled. You'd better pack some **BEEF JERKY** and a **THERMOS OF HOT SOUP,** too.

Okay. You've taken two planes, a logging truck, a snowmobile, and a dogsled with eight big huskies named Alaska, Balto, Chinook, Dancer, Dodger, Elmo, Frost, and Galileo, and you've finally arrived at Elmer's pond. Whew!

The air is so cold, you can see your breath. The ice is so thick, you can walk right out into the middle of the pond. The snow is so thick, you probably won't realize you're even on ice until you hear that little cracking noise.

Uh-oh!

Quick—make a dash for that enormous mound of snow! As you scramble up the side, you might notice sticks poking out here and there. Guess what? You're not climbing up a snowbank. You're climbing up the side of Elmer's lodge.

But where is Elmer?

"Hello?" you might say. "Hellooooo?"

But the forest is quiet. Everywhere the snow lies deep and crisp and smooth. There isn't a single paw mark or beaver-tail trail anywhere. Nobody seems to be around.

So where are Elmer and Irma? Have they flown south with the geese after all?

You might guess that Elmer and Irma are right under your feet, in their lodge with all their children. It's a good guess, but let's think about it for a moment. If we add up all the things you know about beavers and all the things I know about beavers, maybe we can figure out where Elmer is.

I KNOW that Elmer's pond froze back in November, and it will stay frozen until March. That's almost five months.

YOU KNOW that Elmer swims in and out of his lodge by underwater doors.

I KNOW that beavers don't chew secret escape hatches at the top of their lodges.

If we put these three clues together, it certainly explains why you can't see a single beaver trail in the snow. If Elmer and Irma are at home, they've been stuck under the ice for months!

And here are a few more things to consider:

I KNOW an adult beaver needs about 1.5 pounds (0.7 kilograms) of fresh bark per day or about 45 pounds (20 kilograms) per month. Yearlings eat less, and kits even less. It's impossible to know exactly how much food Elmer, Irma, their three yearlings, and four kits will need, but I'm going to say at least 900 pounds (400 kilograms) of branches to survive five months under the ice.

YOU KNOW that's a lot of wood!

YOU ALSO KNOW that Elmer wouldn't gnaw on his lodge. Eating your home isn't a good idea when you're trying to keep your family warm and safe.

Besides, ***YOU KNOW*** Elmer doesn't like old, dead wood.

BUT I KNOW that Elmer has to get 900 pounds of food or his family will starve.

So now that you understand the situation, do you really think Elmer can survive five months under the ice?

Of course he does! What do I keep telling you about beavers? ***THEY'RE RODENT SUPERHEROES!***

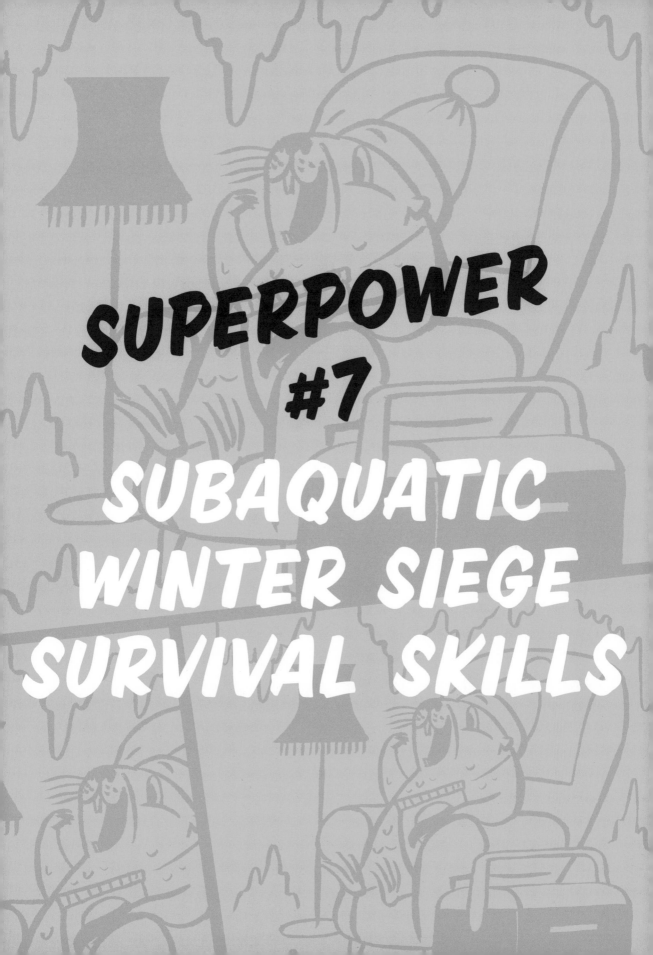

DO YOU KNOW WHAT A SIEGE IS? It's when enemy soldiers circle a castle and just wait. They might send a few arrows over the walls from time to time, but mostly they just wait until the people inside the castle run out of food.

Now, Elmer doesn't have to worry about an army of enemy beavers, but winter can be a cruel enemy, particularly if it locks you under ice for months. Sure, beavers have super-thick fur to keep them warm. And sure, they have a cozy lodge, but none of that matters if you run out of food. So how does Elmer survive the winter siege?

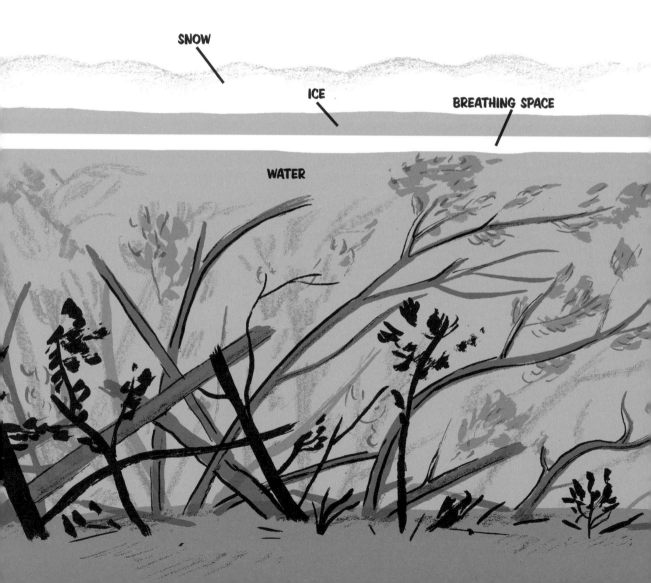

SNOW

ICE

BREATHING SPACE

WATER

At the first sign of frost, Elmer and Irma begin dragging green branches underwater and planting them in the mud near the entrance to their lodge. When I say green branches, I mean young, tasty branches. They keep planting more and more branches until they have an underwater forest. Sometimes the branches take root in the mud and even grow leaves. That's why I call it a ***living larder.*** (As you might know, "larder" is just another word for "pantry," which is just another word for "place to store your food.")

Only the top few inches of pond water freeze. Once they do, Elmer makes a hole in his dam to let out just enough water so there's some breathing space under the ice.

And so, when winter comes and Elmer and his family are under subaquatic siege, they just swim out under the ice, pluck a twig, and drag it back to the lodge, all without worrying about the hungry wolves lurking in the woods, because I'm sure you know that wolves are extra hungry in winter.

The average human eats about 165 pounds (75 kilograms) of food a month. So, for you, your sister, your brother, and your parents to survive five months in your house, you would need 4,125 pounds (1,871 kilograms) of food. Try cramming that into your fridge!

And one more thing. Look down at your feet. What do you see?

Well . . . you probably see carpet. But if you really had taken two planes, a logging truck, a snowmobile, and a dogsled with eight big huskies named Alaska, Balto, Chinook, Dancer, Dodger, Elmo, Frost, and Galileo, and if you really were standing on top of Elmer's lodge, you would see steam. Not a lot, but enough to melt the snow on top of Elmer's lodge. That steam is hot air rising from the warm beaver bodies inside. It lets you know Elmer and his family are at home.

Being locked under ice for months (or even one month, or even a couple of weeks) sounds like a particularly good time to put up your feet and have a long snooze. You might wonder why beavers don't just **hibernate** like chipmunks and bears. I've never asked a beaver, but here is my best guess.

Chipmunks hibernate in holes at the top of trees. Bears hibernate at the back of caves. But beavers are surrounded by water. If the ice and snow suddenly thawed or if the dam broke, poor Elmer would be underwater before he woke up. If I were a beaver, I would want to be on the lookout for trouble.

... THE BIONIC BURROWER!

Okay. While the dogs get harnessed up for the ride home, **HOW ABOUT A LITTLE QUIZ** to pass the time? I'll make it short, because those huskies don't like to wait around once they're ready to go.

QUIZ #3

BELOW IS A PICTURE OF ELMER'S POND. Please draw and clearly label Elmer and his family, the lodge, the living larder, a moose, and where Balto ate your beef jerky.

NOTE: If this is a library book, ***DO NOT DRAW ON THIS PAGE!*** Your librarian isn't going to like that. Not one little bit.

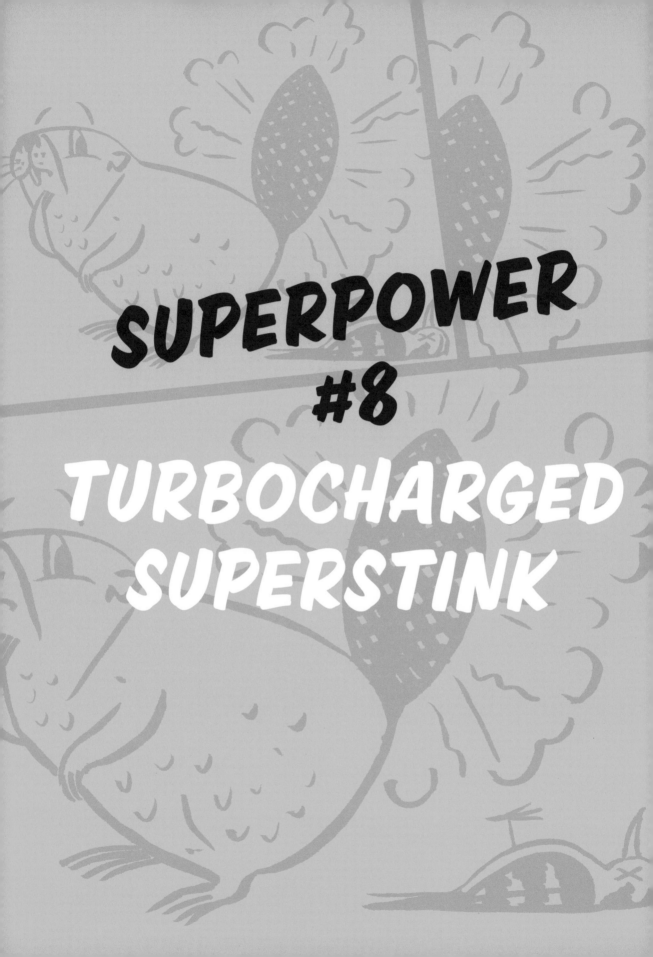

SUPERPOWER
#8

TURBOCHARGED
SUPERSTINK

ELMER AND IRMA WORK HARD to build their home. So I'm sure you'll understand when I say they are very territorial, which means they don't like other beavers coming onto their turf and chewing their trees.

Elmer and Irma don't have a fence around their pond. They don't have locks on the doors. They don't even have doors. But they do have a way of keeping other beavers out. And you'll never believe how stinky it is.

Many animals have scent glands. Scent glands are filled with a musky-smelling oil called **sebum**. Animals and birds use sebum to mark their territory, to find a mate, and even to waterproof their fur and feathers.

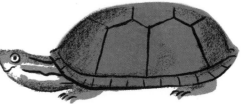

Musk turtles have scent glands around the edge of their shells.

Muskoxen have scent glands in the corners of their eyes.

And beavers . . . well, I guess I have to say it . . . beavers have scent glands near their posterior orifice, which is a very fancy way of saying the opening down below. Beavers have only a single opening down below. It's called a **cloaca**.

But beavers have a second pair of scent organs called *castor sacs*. No other animal has anything like them. Castor sacs are filled with a uniquely smelly beaver oil called castoreum. But *castoreum* isn't just smelly. It has **TURBOCHARGED SUPERSTINK!**

Beaver stink is so musky, ancient doctors believed it was a powerful medicine. They used it for fevers, snakebites, toothaches, vertigo, fainting, and sour belches.

What makes Elmer's castoreum so stinky? It's his diet. You see, many plants have evolved chemicals called *antifeedants* to protect themselves against hungry animals and bugs. Some plants taste bitter. Some plants cause nasty heartburn, and some plants are downright deadly. Most *herbivores* (as plant eaters are called) will just stop eating a bitter plant. A few herbivores have evolved thick stomachs to combat the toxic chemicals. But of course beavers do something extraordinary: beavers turn those toxic plants into the smelliest superpower!

Beavers use castoreum to keep strange beavers away. But they don't just rub their scent on trees as most animals do. Beavers are far classier than that. They're architects, after all! Instead, Elmer and Irma build superstink mud towers. (Well, they're more like mud pies than towers, but let's not get hung up on details.)

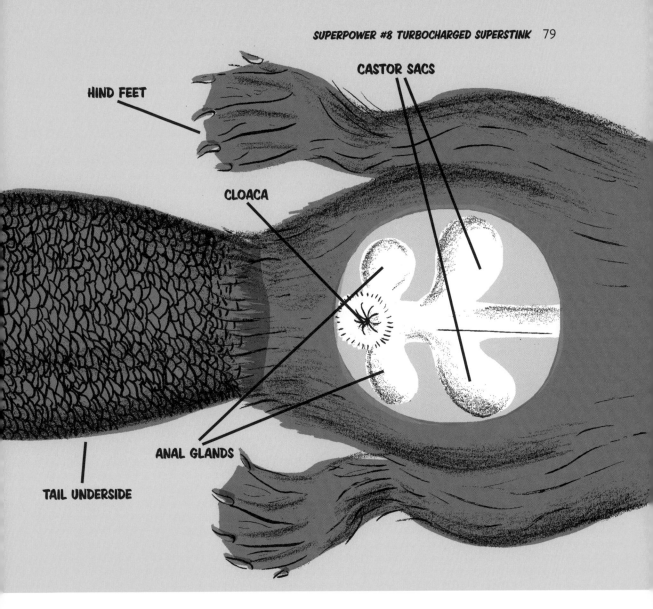

HIND FEET

CASTOR SACS

CLOACA

ANAL GLANDS

TAIL UNDERSIDE

Elmer and Irma build towers all around their pond. First they dive to the bottom of their pond and bring up an armful of mud each. Then they waddle a few steps from the water and plop the mud onto the ground. Sometimes they'll get more and more armloads to make an extra-big mud tower. Then they squirt musky castoreum all over it.

So why do they bother building mud towers? Well, it's always a good idea to put important things up high when the ground is likely to flood. And the towers raise the stink so it can waft farther into the woods to warn any lurking beavers. The wet mud also turbocharges the smell— like how your dog smells extra doggy when he's wet. Who needs a fence and locks when you have *TURBOCHARGED SUPERSTINK?*

SUPERPOWER #9

INDUBITABLE DELUGE DOMINATION

IF YOU VISITED ELMER'S POND in the summertime, you might say something like, "Gosh . . . ain't this quaint?" or "What a charming family of beavers!"

But beavers don't always build their dams in the wilderness. Some beavers build their homes in the middle of town. And when they do, they can cause big problems.

Beavers move into city parks and gnaw down all the newly planted maple trees. Some beavers dam up culverts and wash out roads. Other beavers flood farmers' fields and ruin their crops. When beavers do such things, nobody says, "What a charming family of beavers!" They say, "Those darn beavers are a nuisance!"

Now, you could protect trees by putting iron wire around the trunks. But beavers might build ramps to chew the trees above the wire.

You could break open the dam. But that's like waving a red cape at a bull. Do you remember when I said that leaks drive Elmer crazy? Well, break open Elmer's dam, and he'll go into **SUPER REPAIR OVERDRIVE!** He'll chew down even more trees for the repairs and have the dam strong and solid by morning.

You could trap the beavers and release them far away. But if one beaver thought the area was a pleasant spot to raise a family, then as likely as not, other beavers will move in and begin chewing and munching and flooding all over again.

So what can you do with a nuisance beaver?

YOU BAFFLE THAT BEAVER WITH A BEAVER DECEIVER!

Back in the 1980s, a biologist from Vermont named Skip Lisle was faced with a horde of nuisance beavers. Instead of dynamiting dams or endlessly relocating beavers, he wanted a lasting solution.

He knew that beavers need deep ponds to be safe. But waterlogged basements and soggy fields make humans angry. To keep both beavers safe and humans happy, Skip had the idea of draining just enough water from beaver ponds to stop the flooding but keeping just enough water in the ponds to keep beavers safe and happy.

In 1984, a train traveling between Washington, DC, and Montreal derailed after a flood from a broken beaver dam washed out the railway. Five people died. In Poland, beavers burrowed through the levees along the Vistula River. The floods killed fifteen people. Bad beavers!

The plan sounds like an Easy-Peasy-Lickety-Split-Problem-Solved sort of plan. But it had a big hole, and I'm sure you can guess what it was: Elmer would NEVER allow water to be drained from his pond.

That's when Skip invented his first **BEAVER DECEIVER.** Beaver Deceivers drain water so quietly and so slowly, beavers have no idea it is even happening.

Beaver bafflers come in various shapes and sizes.

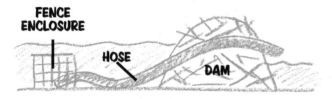

Some look like a large hose: Flexible Pond Leveler™ by Mike Callahan.

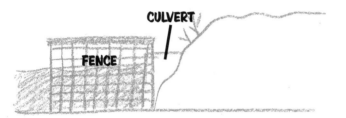

Some look like a cage: Beaver Deceiver™ by Skip Lisle (a trapezoidal beaver fence).

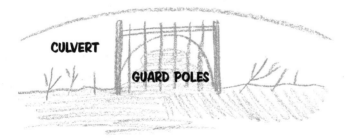

Some are just a row of poles: a culvert guard.

But they all do the same thing: they let humans and beavers live together in happy harmony.

WITH EVERY TREE ELMER CHEWS and every drop of water he
stores in his pond, nibble by nibble, drop by drop, Elmer is changing the
ecology of his forest.

Ecology, as you probably know, is a little word that means big things.
Ecology doesn't just mean the birds, bugs, fish, frogs, trees, ferns, and
mushrooms living in an area. And it doesn't just mean how deep the
snow gets in winter or how many salmon a bear can eat before naptime.
Ecology means all those things all mixed together.

Before Elmer and Irma arrived, the forest was just a forest. But as soon as they began munching trees and damming the river, they quickly turned that ordinary forest into a **STUMP-STUDDED, SOGGY-BOGGY WOODLAND WONDERLAND**—or what scientists call a wetland habitat.

Wetland habitats are home to different creatures than dry forests. Frogs, toads, and salamanders particularly like beaver ponds. Fallen logs and rotting stumps are good homes for ants, centipedes, woodpeckers, and squirrels. Also, because Elmer's lodge is built in the middle of the pond, it makes a perfect spot for geese to lay their eggs, far away from hungry foxes. And, of course, beaver ponds always have water for thirsty animals.

Let's think about this for a moment. When rabbits dig themselves a home, you can twist an ankle in their hole. When deer have a snack, the grass is a lot shorter. But when beavers build their homes and have lunch, they create an entirely new ecosystem for hundreds of other creatures to enjoy. That's a pretty amazing superhero talent!

In fact, it is such an amazing supertalent, scientists have come up with a special name for beavers and other creatures that—by just going about their ordinary business—keep their surrounding ecosystem and all its inhabitants happy and healthy. They are called *keystone species.*

You see, if Elmer and Irma moved to California for more sunshine, their stump-studded, soggy-boggy woodland wonderland would—bit by

bit—turn back into an ordinary forest. And all the frogs, toads, and salamanders, the ants and the centipedes, the woodpeckers, ducks, and herons, the bugs and slugs, not to mention the boggy plants, would all have to find somewhere else to live.

Why are keystone species called keystone species? The name comes from the wedge-shaped piece—known as a keystone—at the top of a stone archway. If the keystone is taken out, the arch will tumble down into a heap of rubbly rock. The same goes for an ecosystem if its keystone species takes an extended holiday.

But wait! It gets even better. Elmer might save your life.

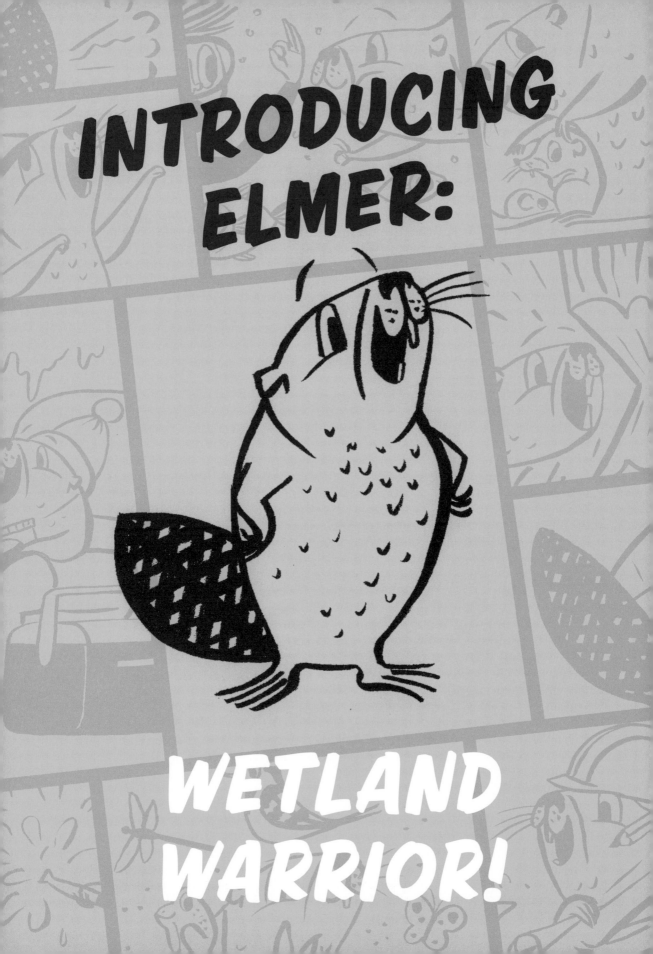

JUST LIKE SUPERMAN, Elmer doesn't just work for his own good. When Elmer puts all his superpowered parts together, he might just save the planet!

You see, being an **UNBEATABLE BOGMAKER** really means that Elmer is a Wetland Warrior. And being a Wetland Warrior means that Elmer doesn't just save water for his family. He saves water for the whole world.

Take spring runoff, for example. When the snow melts in spring, water runs down from the mountains. Spring runoff usually comes hard and fast. The melted snow rushes right down the mountain, through the valley, and out to sea. By the time the summer heat wave hits, all that lovely water is long gone.

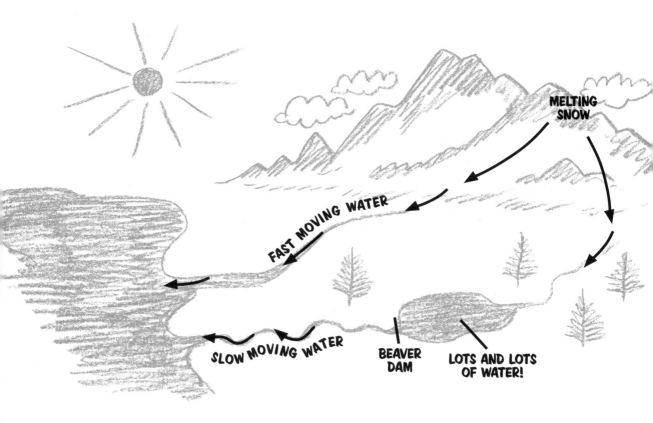

But not in Elmer's pond! Beaver dams help store spring runoff. Dams slow the flow of rivers and allow time for the water to be absorbed into the soil. That means the forest stays moist and green, even during the hot summer months.

And during long and nasty droughts, Elmer and his family go into **WATER MANAGEMENT OVERDRIVE.** They'll make their pond deeper by scooping out mud from the bottom. They'll even dig extra canals to drain as much water as possible into their pond. In fact, beavers do such a super job of collecting water that beaver ponds have nine times more water during droughts than ponds without beavers! Think of all the frogs and salamanders and boggy wetland plants that might shrivel and die without water. When the heat wave arrives, they'll want to be close to a beaver pond.

Farmers might grumble about beavers flooding their fields, but during a scorching summer, a beaver pond might be the only water for their horses and cattle.

And consider this: beavers do such an amazing job of storing water that scientists are putting beavers to work in dried-out places in the hope of rehabilitating the wetlands, which is just a fancy way of saying that scientists are using beavers to bring back the soggy-boggy wonderlands.

The Grand Canyon Trust, for example, has brought beavers back to eighty rivers on the Colorado Plateau, which is one of the driest places in the United States. Scientists have also put beavers back into rivers in Mongolia in the hope of healing the wetlands that dried up after the beavers were gone.

Water means life. Keeping more water around means lusher soil and more green plants in dry places. Lush soil and green plants mean happier animals, cooler air, and healthier people.

Some people even think that beavers make the world so much boggier and greener, happier and healthier, that maybe, just maybe, beavers will help stop climate change. Think of that . . . **ELMER MIGHT SAVE THE WORLD!**

As I said, never underestimate a beaver. Even an ordinary beaver is a **WETLAND WARRIOR!**

But if you think Elmer's amazing, you should hear my story about **ROSALIE THE MOLE . . . BIONIC BURROWER!**

GLOSSARY

ANTIFEEDANTS: nasty chemicals that plants produce to protect themselves against hungry animals. Some antifeedants cause heartburn. Some are strong enough to kill a human.

BEAVER DECEIVER: a clever system to drain just enough water from a beaver pond to prevent flooding the neighbors' houses and crops.

CAPYBARA: a South American **rodent** that looks like an overfed guinea pig.

CARROTING: a chemical technique used to turn beavers' **Unstoppable Fur** into a superpowered beaver felt hat.

CASTOR SACS: a beaver's scent organs that produce **Turbocharged Superstink** known as **castoreum**.

CLOACA: a single opening down below for both kinds of business, if you know what I mean. Most animals (except most mammals) have a cloaca, and what comes out is usually squelchy.

DENTIN: a hard tissue found in teeth.

DROPPINGS: animal poop! Also known as scat.

ECOLOGY: the science of how all the animals and plants and their surrounding natural habitat work together to support life.

ENAMEL: the hard white stuff in your teeth. It is the hardest material in an animal's body. It's harder than bone. It's what makes beaver teeth so strong.

GUARD HAIRS: long, silky animal hairs.

HERBIVORES: plant eaters.

HIBERNATE: to sleep all winter in a cozy fur-lined hole.

INCISORS: the teeth at the very front of your mouth with a sharp, narrow edge. You have four at the top and four at the bottom. Rodents have only two up and two down.

KEYSTONE SPECIES: an animal or plant that supports the health and happiness of its surrounding ecosystem.

KITS: baby beavers. Year-old beavers are called yearlings.

LIVING LARDER: an underwater refrigerator where beavers store their winter food. Scientists sometimes call it a cache.

LODGE: a beaver's home.

NICTITATING MEMBRANE: Underwater Goggle Greatness! A transparent eyelid that protects beaver eyeballs from underwater mud and grit.

NOCTURNAL: sleeping all day, busy all night.

RODENT: the beast that gnaws!

ROUGHAGE: Super-high-fiber food like wood, grass, and hay.

SEBUM: a musky-smelling oil.

UNDERBARK: the young and tasty (at least, tasty to beavers) green bark growing underneath a tree's outer woody bark.

UNDERFUR: those short, thick, gray, and fuzzy hairs found underneath the long, silky **guard hairs.** Your cat has them. So does your dog. But you don't.

FURTHER BEAVER READING

CHECK OUT SOME MORE GREAT BEAVER BOOKS:

Beavers by Gail Gibbons (Holiday House, 2014)

Beavers and Other Animals with Amazing Teeth by Susan LaBella (Children's Press, 2005)

The Beavers' Busy Year by Mary Holland (Sylvan Dell Publishing, 2014)

Welcome to the World of Beavers by Diane Swanson (Walrus Books, 2004)

AND IF YOU'RE FEELING COURAGEOUSLY CURIOUS, THESE BOOKS GET SERIOUS:

The American Beaver and His Works by Lewis H. Morgan (1868)

Beaver by Rachel Poliquin (Reaktion Books, 2015)

The Beaver Manifesto by Glynnis Hood (Rocky Mountain Books, 2011)

Fur, Fortune, and Empire: The Epic History of the Fur Trade in America by Eric Jay Dolin (W. W. Norton, 2010)

In Beaver World by Enos Mills (1913)

AND A COUPLE OF GREAT BEAVER WEBSITES:

Kids' Zone at the Scottish Beaver Trial: The official site of the beaver introductions into Scotland. www.scottishbeavers.org.uk/beaver-facts/kids-zone

Worth A Dam: An organization in California dedicated to inspiring and educating urban communities on the benefits of coexisting with beavers. www.MartinezBeavers.org